UNCOVERING THE STORY OF YOUR GRANDPARENT'S LIFE

199 QUESTIONS FOR GRANDMA AND GRANDPA TO TRANSFORM THEIR EXPERIENCES INTO A MEMOIR

THE POSITIVITY POLICY

CONTENTS

FOR NORM AND SHIRLEY (MOMMA
AND POPS)

*No matter how many stories you tell your grandkids, we're always
excited to hear the next one.*
You're loved more than you'll ever know.

A LITTLE EXTRA BONUS FOR YOU!

FREE GIFT FOR OUR READERS

The practical checklist of

33 Stupid-Simple Negative Habits

and effortless suggestions to overcome

WWW.POSITIVITYPOLICY.NET

Get a jump on eliminating some of your negative habits and building your confidence with this checklist. Visit this link:

www.PositivityPolicy.info

INTRODUCTION

When thinking of your grandparents, it's easy to feel like you really know them, but do you know all of the fun details? Caring about your family can easily turn into planning and attending family events, taking care of family emergencies, and helping each other out during times of need. It's far too easy to be around each other and talking about random things without learning more. You're not alone! Life is busy, there are distractions galore, and with all of the attention that your personal demands require, sometimes it's hard to be focused during family time.

Thankfully, now you have this nifty book of 199 questions to ask your grandparents during these times. You will be shocked at some of the answers, you'll cry with some of them, but more importantly, you will get to know them more in-depth with more meaningful conversation. Time is a crazy thing, and most people would always take more if they had the option, so have fun picking a few questions every time you get to sit down and talk with your grandparents and lock those memories away for forever.

The impact of someone's grandparents is so much deeper than the surface. They influenced and raised the parents. They were the support that helped those parents raise their children, which could be you! These are just a few small things that inspired the questions included for you to ask. Now get to it! Pick up your phone, schedule a facetime or zoom call, or simply pay your grandpa or grandma a visit and start logging memories.

PERSONAL / FAMILY

1. Were you named after a particular family member, or does your name have a special meaning?

_____

_____

_____

_____

_____

2. Do you have a nickname that your siblings or friends call you? How did you get the nickname?

_____

_____

_____

_____

_____

3. What is the funniest nickname of a relative? How did they get it?

_____

_____

_____

_____

_____

4. Who was the jokester/trickster of your family growing up?

_____

_____

_____

_____

_____

5. What's your favorite family story to tell?

_____

_____

_____

_____

_____

6. What would you say makes your family unique from other families?

_____

_____

_____

_____

_____

7. If you had to create a family motto, what would it be?

_____

_____

_____

_____

_____

8. Did you practice religion growing up? What are some memories of this?

_____

_____

_____

_____

_____

9. What were the occupations of your parents?

_____

_____

_____

_____

_____

10. What do you remember most about your mother?

_____

_____

_____

_____

_____

11. What do you remember most about your father?

_____

_____

_____

_____

_____

12. What do you remember most about your grandparents?

_____

_____

_____

_____

_____

13. How did your parents pass away?

_____

_____

_____

_____

_____

14. What are your memories of them passing? How did you get through it?

_____

_____

_____

_____

_____

15. Are there other family members that stand out in your memory? What makes them so memorable to you?

_____

_____

_____

_____

_____

16. How many children were in your family? What are all their names?

_____

_____

_____

_____

17. What was a typical family dinner like? Who did the cooking? What were your favorite meals?

_____

_____

_____

_____

_____

18. What were your parent's careers?

_____

_____

_____

_____

19. What kind of car did the family drive? (make, model, color?)

_____

_____

_____

_____

_____

20. Who are/were the best cooks in the family? What did they cook?

_____

_____

_____

_____

_____

THE EARLY YEARS

21. Where were you born?

_____

_____

_____

_____

_____

22. What is your very oldest memory you still have?

_____

_____

_____

_____

_____

23. What are the earliest memories of your first home?

_____

_____

_____

_____

_____

24. What town did you grow up in? If you moved, where to? Tell me about these places!

_____

_____

_____

_____

_____

25. What are memories of other homes and places you lived?

_____

_____

_____

_____

_____

26. How did your family spend time together when you were young?

_____

_____

_____

_____

27. What was your first pet? What was their name?

_____

_____

_____

_____

_____

28. What was your favorite pet? What was their name?

_____

_____

_____

_____

_____

29. What was your favorite holiday when you were a child, and why?

_____

_____

_____

_____

_____

30. What is the most important lesson that your parents taught you?

_____

_____

_____

_____

_____

31. What did you do to celebrate birthdays?

_____

_____

_____

_____

_____

32. Who was your best friend as a child, and how did you meet?

_____

_____

_____

_____

_____

33. What were your favorite toys as a child?

_____

_____

_____

_____

_____

34. What was your favorite joke as a child?

_____

_____

_____

_____

_____

35. Did you ever do anything naughty as a kid?

_____

_____

_____

_____

_____

36. What is different about growing up today than when you were a child?

_____

_____

_____

_____

_____

37. What were your favorite toys or things to do in your teens?

_____

_____

_____

_____

_____

38. What games did you play as a kid?

_____

_____

_____

_____

_____

39. What was your neighborhood like?

_____

_____

_____

_____

_____

40. What was your favorite television show as a child?

_____

_____

_____

_____

_____

41. What's your favorite special memory of growing up with your brother(s) or sister(s)?

_____

_____

_____

_____

_____

42. Did you have any childhood diseases? How did that affect your childhood?

_____

_____

_____

_____

_____

43. When you were young, did you ever collect anything? What was it and why?

_____

_____

_____

_____

_____

44. What were your daily household chores growing up?

_____

_____

_____

_____

_____

45. What was your bedtime as a child?

_____

_____

_____

_____

_____

AS YOU GOT OLDER

46. What was your favorite subject, and who was your favorite teacher in school?

_____

_____

_____

_____

_____

47. What subject(s) were you strongest in?

_____

_____

_____

_____

_____

48. What was your personality at school? (shy, outgoing, class clown?)

_____

_____

_____

_____

_____

49. What was the school subject you struggled with the most? Why?

_____

_____

_____

_____

_____

50. Was there a teacher that you particularly disliked? Why?

_____

_____

_____

_____

_____

51. What did you do with your friends for fun when you were young?

_____

_____

_____

_____

_____

52. What did your family do for fun when you were a kid?

_____

_____

_____

_____

_____

53. Did you and your friends have a special place to hang out? Can you tell me about that place?

_____

_____

_____

_____

_____

54. What did you wear to school? (elementary, high school, college?)

_____

_____

_____

_____

_____

55. How would people who knew you in high school describe you?

_____

_____

_____

_____

_____

56. Who was your best friend in high school? Where did you meet?

_____

_____

_____

_____

_____

57. Were you involved in any school sports or clubs? Did you receive any awards?

_____

_____

_____

_____

_____

58. What were some fads from your youth? Popular hairstyles? Clothes? Which of these was your favorite/least favorite?

_____

_____

_____

_____

_____

59. Did you get an allowance? How much was it, and what did you spend your money on? (did you save it?)

_____

_____

_____

_____

_____

60. When did you open your first bank account?

_____

_____

_____

_____

61. Did you ever get into trouble with your friends? Tell the story!

_____

_____

_____

_____

_____

62. Were there any race, gender, or social challenges where you grew up? How did this affect you?

_____

_____

_____

_____

_____

63. What was the first movie you saw in a theater? How old were you?

_____

_____

_____

_____

64. What was the make, model, color, and year of the first car you ever owned?

_____

_____

_____

_____

65. How did you earn money for that first car? Did you save your money? How long did it take you? Did your parents help you out?

_____

_____

_____

_____

_____

66. When was the maddest you ever made your parents? What did you do to make them so aggravated?

_____

_____

_____

_____

_____

67. Did you have a curfew, and what time was it? Did you ever miss curfew?

_____

_____

_____

_____

68. What was your first date like? Who did you go with? Where did you go?

_____

_____

_____

_____

_____

69. What did you do right after high school? (Did you move out and start working, go to the military, continued education?)

_____

_____

_____

_____

_____

RELATIONSHIPS

70. How did you meet Grandma/Grandpa?

_____

_____

_____

_____

_____

71. What qualities do you remember liking about them?

_____

_____

_____

_____

_____

72. What about them made you fall in love?

_____

_____

_____

_____

73. How did you know that they were the one for you?

_____

_____

_____

_____

_____

74. What did your parents think when they first met
Grandma/Grandpa?

_____

_____

_____

_____

_____

75. How long did you date? What was that like?

_____

_____

_____

_____

_____

76. What was your marriage proposal like?

_____

_____

_____

_____

_____

77. Where was your wedding? How many people attended? Tell me about the ceremony.

_____

_____

_____

_____

_____

78. What was the theme or decoration style of your wedding?

_____

_____

_____

_____

79. Who was your maid of honor or best man? How did you decide?

_____

_____

_____

_____

_____

80. Did you have a honeymoon? Where did you go? How was your experience?

_____

_____

_____

_____

_____

81. What did you find the most challenging during the first years of being married?

_____

_____

_____

_____

_____

82. What was the most memorable gesture Grandma/Grandpa ever did for you? Why did it mean so much to you?

_____

_____

_____

83. What was the most memorable gesture you made for Grandma/Grandpa? What inspired you to do that for them? How did it go?

_____

_____

_____

_____

_____

84. What was/has been one of the biggest struggles you've overcome together?

_____

_____

_____

_____

85. What was the most significant disagreement you ever got into? How did it start, and how did you resolve it?

_____

_____

_____

86. Were there any rough times? What was your secret for staying together?

_____

_____

_____

_____

_____

87. What is your favorite anniversary that you've ever celebrated? What made it special?

_____

_____

_____

_____

88. What is your favorite quality in Grandma/Grandpa?

_____

_____

_____

_____

89. What was one of the most annoying tendencies that Grand-ma/Grandpa did? How did you learn to live with it?

_____

_____

_____

_____

_____

90. If you've been divorced, what caused that?

_____

_____

_____

_____

_____

91. Have you been married more than once? How did you decide you were ready again?

_____

_____

_____

_____

_____

JOBS / CAREERS

92. What did you do for your first job?

_____

_____

_____

_____

_____

93. What did you want to be when you grew up?

_____

_____

_____

_____

_____

94. How did you decide on a career?

_____

_____

_____

_____

_____

95. If you changed careers in life, what made you decide to change course midway through life?

_____

_____

_____

_____

_____

96. Who was the worst boss you ever had? What made them so bad?

_____

_____

_____

_____

_____

97. Who was the best boss you ever had? What made them so great?

_____

_____

_____

_____

_____

98. What is a job you always wanted to have but never got a chance to work?

_____

_____

_____

_____

_____

99. What factors do you think are the most important when choosing what to do for a living?

_____

_____

_____

_____

_____

100. Who was one of your biggest mentors? What did they do to influence you and make a difference in your life?

_____

_____

_____

_____

_____

CHILDREN / PARENTING

101. When did you know you were ready to have children?

_____

_____

_____

_____

_____

102. How did you find out you were going to be a parent for the first time?

_____

_____

_____

_____

_____

103. How many children did you have altogether?

_____

_____

_____

_____

104. How did you choose the names for your children?

_____

_____

_____

_____

_____

105. What are their names, birthplaces, birthdays?

_____

_____

_____

_____

_____

106. What were your children's personalities like when they were young?

_____

_____

_____

_____

_____

107. How would you describe their personalities as they grew up?

_____

_____

_____

_____

_____

108. What are your children doing now as adults? What careers, do they have children themselves, where do they live?

_____

_____

_____

_____

_____

109. When you started trying for children, did you have a plan for how many? What is that number and why?

_____

_____

_____

_____

110. Did you want boys or girls? Did you get what you wanted?

_____

_____

_____

_____

111. Looking back, would you have tried for (more) children? Why or why not?

_____

_____

_____

_____

_____

112. Are there any funny or unusual things your children did?

_____

_____

_____

_____

113. Were you strict or lenient as a parent? Give me an example!

_____

_____

_____

_____

_____

114. What was the most challenging moment as a parent, and how did you get through it?

_____

_____

_____

_____

_____

115. What's something your kid(s) did that made you the most nervous/scared? How did it turn out?

_____

_____

_____

_____

_____

116. What were some of the proudest moments you had as a parent?

_____

_____

_____

_____

_____

117. What was/were one/some of the proudest moments you had as a grandparent?

_____

_____

_____

_____

_____

118. Who in your life was the most supportive of you when you first became a parent?

_____

_____

_____

_____

_____

119. What was one of the most challenging moments as a new parent, and how did you get through it?

_____

_____

_____

_____

120. When your kids turned into adults and moved out, how did that feel?

_____

_____

_____

_____

_____

121. What is one thing you learned from your parents that you tried your hardest to do as a parent yourself?

_____

_____

_____

_____

122. What is one thing your parents did that you swore you would never do when you became a parent?

_____

_____

_____

_____

123. Of all the things you learned from your parents, which do you feel was the most valuable?

_____

_____

_____

_____

_____

124. What is the most rewarding thing about being a parent/grandparent?

_____

_____

_____

_____

VACATIONS / TRAVEL

125. What was your first vacation or trip? Where did you go? How was it?

_____

_____

_____

_____

_____

126. What all states/countries have you traveled to in your life?

_____

_____

_____

_____

_____

127. Do you have any scary memories from traveling?

_____

_____

_____

_____

_____

128. What is the longest trip you've ever been on? How long did you travel for? What inspired you to take the journey?

_____

_____

_____

_____

_____

129. What is your favorite city you've visited? Why?

_____

_____

_____

_____

_____

130. Out of the places you've lived throughout your life, which was your favorite and why?

_____

_____

_____

_____

_____

131. Do you have a favorite family vacation memory?

_____

_____

_____

_____

_____

132. What is the most beautiful place you have ever visited? Who was there with you and when did you go?

_____

_____

_____

_____

_____

133. If you could travel anywhere in the world, where would it be and why?

_____

_____

_____

_____

_____

134. What is the most interesting place you've visited? What made it that way?

_____

_____

_____

_____

135. What is somewhere everyone always talks about, but you never had any interest in ever visiting?

_____

_____

_____

_____

_____

FAVORITES

136. What's your favorite funny family story?

_____

_____

_____

_____

_____

137. What is your favorite book? When did you first read it?

_____

_____

_____

_____

_____

138. What is your favorite movie? When and where did you first watch it?

_____

_____

_____

_____

_____

139. What is your favorite song? When and where did you first hear it?

_____

_____

_____

_____

_____

140. What is your favorite sport/athlete? What's your favorite memory of them?

_____

_____

_____

_____

_____

141. What is your favorite board game? What's your favorite experience playing it?

_____

_____

_____

_____

_____

142. What's your favorite card game? What's your favorite experience playing it?

_____

_____

_____

_____

143. What's your favorite sweet treat of all time? Where did you get it from?

_____

_____

_____

_____

_____

144. What's your favorite drink of all time? (soda, tea, coffee, alcohol doesn't matter! Where did you first discover it?)

_____

_____

_____

_____

145. What's your favorite restaurant? What made/makes it so amazing?

_____

_____

_____

_____

146. What is your favorite season? What makes it the best to you?

_____

_____

_____

_____

_____

147. What are your favorite family recipes?

_____

_____

_____

_____

_____

148. What is your favorite animal?

_____

_____

_____

_____

_____

149. What is your favorite candy?

_____

_____

_____

_____

_____

150. What is your favorite color?

_____

_____

_____

_____

_____

151. What is your favorite type of cookie?

_____

_____

_____

_____

_____

152. What is your favorite flower?

153. What is your favorite flavor of ice cream?

154. What is your favorite instrument?

155. What is your favorite sport?

_____

_____

_____

_____

_____

156. What's your favorite holiday meal?

_____

_____

_____

_____

157. What's your favorite holiday dessert?

_____

_____

_____

_____

_____

158. What's your favorite holiday-themed music/singer?

_____

_____

_____

_____

_____

159. What is your favorite holiday? Why?

_____

_____

_____

_____

160. What are some of your favorite memories from holidays?

_____

_____

_____

_____

_____

HISTORICAL EVENTS

161. What do you think are the most significant inventions in your lifetime?

_____

_____

_____

_____

_____

162. Do you remember the first time you saw a television, car, plane? Describe that feeling!

_____

_____

_____

_____

_____

163. Do you have memories of your family talking about world events and politics?

_____

_____

_____

_____

164. What are your memories of major world events? (WWII, Pearl Harbor, September 11, Vietnam war, etc.)

_____

_____

_____

_____

165. What was the most exciting event that happened to your recollection? (Election, the man on the moon, favorite athlete winning a championship, records being broken, etc.)

_____

_____

_____

_____

_____

166. Do you remember living through a tough financial time? (Great Depression, for example) How did you get through it?

_____

_____

_____

_____

_____

167. Did you serve in the military? What branch? What rank? When?

_____

_____

_____

_____

168. Did you ever fight in a war-time battle? Where?

_____

_____

_____

_____

_____

HOLIDAYS

169. What Holidays do you have traditions for? What are they?

_____

_____

_____

_____

_____

170. Are there any special dishes you used to or continue to make or eat for certain holidays?

_____

_____

_____

_____

_____

171. Are there any unique family heirlooms you have inherited? What special meanings or feelings do they give you?

_____

_____

_____

_____

172. What's the most surprising gift you've ever received? Why was it so surprising to you?

_____

_____

_____

_____

173. What's the worst gift you've ever received? Why was it so bad?

_____

_____

_____

_____

_____

174. What's the best gift you've ever received? What made it special?

_____

_____

_____

_____

_____

WHERE YOU'RE AT NOW

175. Who are your closest friends to this day? Which one have you had the longest?

_____

_____

_____

_____

_____

176. What's one of the most embarrassing things that's happened to you?

_____

_____

_____

_____

_____

177. What kind of books do you like to read?

_____

_____

_____

_____

_____

178. What were the most challenging choices you ever had to make?

_____

_____

_____

_____

_____

179. What is the best decision you've ever made?

_____

_____

_____

_____

_____

180. Tell me about a challenging situation where you had to say "no."

_____

_____

_____

_____

_____

181. Were there any events that vastly changed the course of your life?

_____

_____

_____

_____

_____

182. What person had the most considerable impact on the course of your life? How?

_____

_____

_____

_____

_____

183. What's something you can tell me about yourself that would surprise me?

_____

_____

_____

_____

184. What's your best advice on how to handle stress?

_____

_____

_____

_____

185. What was the most stressful experience you've experienced?

_____

_____

_____

_____

_____

186. Have you ever been a victim of a crime? If so, what was it? How did it happen? Were you okay?

_____

_____

_____

_____

_____

187. Have you been in a severe accident? How did it happen? Was everyone okay?

_____

_____

_____

_____

188. Has anyone ever saved your life? If yes, how did they do it?

_____

_____

_____

_____

_____

189. What was the scariest thing you've ever lived through?

_____

_____

_____

_____

190. What was the funniest practical joke you ever played on someone?

_____

_____

_____

_____

_____

191. What were/are some of your favorite activities or hobbies as an adult?

_____

_____

_____

_____

_____

192. Who is the most famous person you've ever met? What was that experience like?

_____

_____

_____

_____

193. Have you won any special awards or prizes as an adult? What were they for? Which one made you the proudest?

_____

_____

_____

194. What organizations or groups have you been a member of as an adult?

_____

_____

_____

_____

_____

195. What are some things that you enjoy doing now?

_____

_____

_____

_____

_____

196. What are your hopes for your family?

_____

_____

_____

_____

197. What's something that you learned later in life that surprised you that you can share with me?

_____

_____

_____

_____

_____

198. What values do you hope get passed down to the younger generations in your family?

_____

_____

_____

_____

_____

199. What is the one thing you most want people to remember about you?

_____

_____

_____

SO...

WHAT DID YOU LEARN?

You did it! After talking with your grandparents, Grandma, or Grandpa and asking them all of these different questions about different times of their life would be a great time to do a little reflecting.

What lessons did you learn that you will forever hold on to? What memories were renewed that you forgot? What did you learn that inspired you to model some of your behavior or future actions? How do you feel having had all of that valuable time with them?

The following page will ask you about a review, but directly following, you will find ten pages for you to jot down any reflections that you would want to keep in this book along with the other memories you've captured.

LEAVE A REVIEW

Being an independent author duo with a smaller marketing budget to spend, reviews make a world of difference in our success.

If you gained value from this book (or simply enjoyed it), we would be extremely grateful if you leave your honest feedback in the form of a review where you purchased it.

We love hearing from our readers and personally read every review and take that feedback seriously.

REFLECTIONS

_____

_____

_____

_____

_____

_____

_____

_____

_____

_____

_____

_____

_____

_____

_____

_____

_____

_____

_____

_____

_____

_____

_____

_____

_____

_____

_____

REFLECTIONS